Leadership

The Compendium Of Essential Knowledge For
Achieving Success In Your Emerging Leadership Role

*(Maximize Your Organization's Capabilities With
Thoughtful Leadership And Fairness)*

Mathieu Deschamps

TABLE OF CONTENT

Don't Lead By Intimidation 1

The Inaugural Principle Of Motion Established By Sir Isaac Newton: 4

Business Analogy And 4

Interpretation 4

How To Influence People? 8

Systematic Thinking 15

Learning To Think Systematically 24

Improving Your Social Intelligence 28

Who Are You? 46

The Confident Leader 70

Non-Verbal Communication Can Facilitate Interpersonal Interactions. 75

Management Skills 83

The Importance Of Interpersonal Connections And Proficient Verbal And Non-Verbal Exchange 96

The Impact Of Leadership Styles" Or "The Consequences Of Different Leadership Approaches 103

The Leader And Motives 110

Equip Your Followers For Achieving Success 139

Increase Influence 156

Transforming Pessimistic Thoughts Into Optimistic Perspectives 165

Don't Lead By Intimidation

By embracing a mindset of self-correction, you can attain desired outcomes. To put it differently, the intimidating nature of a lion does not necessarily manifest solely through roaring. You would experience fear if you were encountered by a lion in its natural habitat. Would it be necessary to emit a substantial sound in order to capture your attention? I am of the opinion that it is unlikely. I believe that individuals possessing sound reasoning would be unsettled merely upon witnessing it. Intimidation only leads to temporary rewards. Demonstrate a level of maturity in your role as a leader by empowering individuals rather than exercising dominion over them. A well-executed coaching session will yield significantly greater benefits for both yourself and your team member as compared to resorting to a session filled with shouting. Engaging in verbal outbursts or diminishing the value of an employee's contributions can result in the cultivation of negative feelings and a significant increase in employee attrition rates. Maintain composure during all interactions. Indeed, it is undeniable that a leader is expected to possess a certain degree of authority, sufficient to communicate to their subordinates that they are not easily taken advantage of. Find the balance. Certain leaders resort to instilling fear as a means of exerting influence due to their own inherent apprehensions. They engage in this behavior as a precautionary measure against potential adverse repercussions originating from higher authorities. Do not become one of these leaders. Adopt the role of a mentor, rather than a tyrant, in the process of cultivating a strong team. Bear in mind: employing forceful tactics may have proven effective during the era of primitive humans and ancient reptiles. Thankfully, we have progressed beyond such methods! Should you presently employ fear as a means of leadership, it will necessitate dedication, assistance, and a substantial amount of time, but transformation is achievable. Get a mentor, ask your boss for help and start reading some good books on leadership. According to Brian Tracy, it is advisable to allocate 3% of your income towards advancing your professional and personal growth. I will provide further elaboration on this matter at a later point in time.

The Inaugural Principle Of Motion Established By Sir Isaac Newton:

Business Analogy And Interpretation

According to the principles of Physics, Newton's first law holds that an object will persist in its state of rest or uniform motion unless acted upon by an external force. To alter the state entails the generation of acceleration, necessitating the application of an external force. The outcome could vary depending on the orientation and application of external force, potentially resulting in either positive acceleration or deceleration of the state. By applying analogical derivations, it is possible to establish a correlation between corporate operations and the continuous growth of the profit rate. In the event that the machinery, manpower, departments, and protocols remain unchanged, it is likely that we will experience a consistent profit margin, albeit potentially diminished. However, by incorporating and maintaining the machinery, improving the skill set of our workforce, conducting regular departmental audits, and continually adjusting protocols based on periodic observations (with a focus on adopting a forward-thinking approach, embracing technological advancements, and incorporating insights from management and consumers), we can ensure a consistent upward trajectory in our profit margin.

Psychological perspective: The concept of "cognitive dissonance" is employed in psychological discourse to elucidate the phenomenon wherein individuals resiliently uphold their existing system of beliefs despite encountering new observations that suggest a need for change. Their 'cognition' remains fixed. That represents an individual's resistance to change and willingness to embrace new circumstances. In the event that such a mindset prevails amongst members of the corporate workforce, the growth potential of the corporations will inevitably be stymied. In a corporate setting, it is imperative to consistently review and update various aspects such as operations, departments, and business protocols.

CORPORATE INSIGHT: The presence of inertia, regardless of its magnitude or location, can have detrimental effects. There ought to be proactive efforts towards 'change engineering' in order to facilitate ongoing progress. There should be a deliberate implementation of 'change engineering' to promote continual development. It is imperative to engage in 'change engineering' as a means to ensure steady advancement. There needs to be a concerted focus on 'change engineering' to foster continuous development.

How To Influence People?

An indication of effective leadership is the leader's capacity to exert influence over individuals. This chapter will elucidate several highly efficacious tactics for enhancing one's influence as a leader.

Display a sincere curiosity about individuals" "Exhibit a genuine concern for others' well-being" "Manifest a true inquisitiveness towards other individuals

Your magnitude of impact is primarily determined by your capacity to establish meaningful connections with individuals in your immediate environment. Do you allocate time to demonstrate genuine interest in what others are expressing? Demonstrate sincere interest in your members. This demonstrates your genuine concern for their emotions and perspectives, while also acknowledging and appreciating their valuable contributions to the group. Once you facilitate the establishment of such sentiments, it becomes effortless to exert influence upon them, prompting them to readily conform to your guidance.

Build a harmonious relationship
Ensure that your presence instills a sense of ease and comfort among your fellow members. Rather than fostering hostility and apprehension, it is imperative to cultivate an atmosphere wherein your supporters perceive you as an accessible and approachable leader. Engage in occasional social interactions with them. During designated periods of rest, endeavor to engage in conversation with individuals or exchange anecdotes with them. This greatly facilitates the development of trust within your group and fosters a sense of comfort among your members. Once they have developed a sense of familiarity and ease in your presence, exerting influence over them will cease to pose a significant challenge.

Build a good reputation

It is unreasonable to anticipate individuals to comply with one's guidance if one possesses a poor reputation. You have the potential to become a highly influential leader if your followers perceive you as possessing unwavering credibility and unwavering honesty. Maintain transparency and integrity in your interactions with your team. Refrain from engaging in deceptive practices or concealing pertinent information from them. Upon their discovery of your deception, the restoration of their trust shall prove arduous. Becoming a person of influence in leadership will remain unattainable unless one manages to earn their trust and belief in oneself.

Provide positive feedback
Rather than placing emphasis on the errors made by your members, strive to identify the positive aspects of their performance, even if they are seemingly insignificant. Allocate investment towards fostering and empowering your members, as opposed to

employing conditions and deterrents. Through the consistent offering of proactive affirmation, your constituents are able to perceive your favorable attributes and well-intentioned motives, thereby fostering a greater propensity to place trust in your guidance and leadership.

Admit your mistakes
Many leaders struggle with acknowledging their own shortcomings. Typically, individuals in such circumstances commonly attribute their faults to external factors, operating under the assumption that their elevated status renders them incapable of erring. Strive to steer clear of these types of leadership roles. Exhibit the qualities of a leader who is self-aware and readily acknowledges his own mistakes. By openly acknowledging your errors, you effectively convey your genuine concern for your constituents. Additionally, you are demonstrating a profound understanding of the impact

that your conduct and errors can have on the entire collective.

Be visible

Outstanding and proficient leaders are those who possess a visible presence, evident to their members and followers, rather than merely being heard. Many contemporary leaders lack visibility to their constituents due to their exceedingly busy schedules. A portion of individuals depart their place of work without conducting a thorough assessment of the well-being of their subordinates. Certain leaders, perhaps even concealing themselves within their offices, exhibit a tendency to evade interpersonal interactions.

It is imperative to modify this behavior. As a leader, it is imperative for you to acknowledge that the success of your organization is contingent upon the collective endeavors of your group. Spend time in their company and make occasional appearances in their presence. Sometimes, a friendly hello to your team is enough to boost their morale.

Act on things quickly

If you demonstrate prompt action to your members, you have the potential to become an impactful leader. Please ensure timely response is given. It is important to be mindful that by extensively deliberating, deferring action, or engaging in procrastination when faced with a challenging decision, you are effectively conveying a negative impression to your constituents.

In order to assume a position of influential leadership, it is imperative to promptly initiate action, as your subordinates anticipate your decisive judgment. This can serve as a powerful source of motivation for your members. Additionally, this can foster an increase in their confidence and bolster their trust in your competence.

There are numerous avenues by which a leader can exert influence over individuals. Outlined earlier are some of the most efficient options. After following these simple steps, you will notice that more and more people are believing in you, and are becoming more willing to follow you.

Systematic Thinking

The methodology utilized to achieve our desired outcomes exceeds conventional strategic approaches and thus shall be labeled as systematic cognition. In order to foster a fundamental aspect of systematic thinking, it is imperative to recognize and give due consideration to both one's own internal representations and those of others. It is crucial that we acknowledge the intricate relationship between our internal perceptions and mindset, and how they correspond with our external behavior and ensuing outcomes.

Efficient systematic thinking is cultivated by incorporating a diverse range of critical thinking abilities into one's functional repertoire. By employing strategic approaches, individuals with a propensity for systematic thinking are able to effectively predict, evaluate, and exert control over future events. In order to improve our capacity for critical thinking, it is essential to first ascertain and fully grasp the diverse factors involved. Subsequently, we must allocate our focus to each constituent while ultimately synthesizing them in a manner that is congruent with our unique preferences, principles, and goals. To establish the associations between your internal condition, perceptions, and outward actions, it is crucial to partake in a process of introspection by means of the subsequent investigations:

What is my current state?

What preliminary observations can be made regarding the subject matter?

How do the specific elements of the matter relate to my personal circumstances?

How have my actions impacted the advancement of this process?

What influence has the process exerted on my behaviors?

What methods do I plan to utilize in order to exert a substantial impact on the prevailing system or situation?

Is the current procedure indeed encountering a dearth of effectiveness? On several occasions, the operations have displayed exceptional effectiveness, albeit not in line with our initial anticipations.

Are my internal representations and state the root cause of any difficulties encountered?

Might the existing circumstances or challenges be ascribed to the fundamental factor affecting my emotional wellbeing?

What is the intrinsic value or importance of this specific circumstance?

Have prior instances of this issue or analogous issues been dealt with?

If that is indeed true, may I inquire about the steps taken to rectify the situation?

The human cerebral cortex consists of two discrete hemispheres, namely the left hemisphere and the right hemisphere. It is widely held that each hemisphere carries the responsibility of regulating distinctly different cognitive abilities. Our cerebral left hemispheres are responsible for overseeing our rational and logical cognitive processes, whereas creativity predominantly resides in the right hemisphere. Each person has a predisposition for a specific cognitive style; some individuals demonstrate a predilection for creative thinking, which corresponds to the right hemisphere, while others tend to favor a more logical and conventional approach typically associated with the left hemisphere. An essential element of systematic thinking entails effectively utilizing the cognitive capacities of both cerebral hemispheres, proficiently alternating between divergent and convergent thinking as a means to effectively maneuver intricate circumstances. There are a multitude of strategies available that can augment our aptitude.

New Stimulations

Whenever we extend our personal limitations or embark on unprecedented undertakings, our rational and creative abilities invariably cooperate.

Unprecedented conditions prompt our innovative thinking, while simultaneously involving our logical reasoning to assess possible risks and opportunities. All of these events unfold swiftly and naturally. Participating in unfamiliar and challenging situations can effectively enhance cognitive adaptability while also providing a pleasurable encounter.

Please direct your attention to the most recent concepts.

Inspiration can be found ubiquitously, often appearing in unexpected forms. It is of utmost importance to exercise due diligence in capturing and consolidating contemporary concepts. Innovation is the catalyst for profound change, thus it is prudent to encourage your team to exhibit unwavering dedication towards the pursuit of original concepts. By taking this course of action, you will ensure that you remain at the vanguard of advancement.

Increase your knowledge

Merely possessing experience is inadequate in acquiring mastery in the realm of problem-solving. Gaining knowledge enhances our ability to formulate outcomes. Having an extensive breadth of knowledge and a keenly imaginative outlook are highly valued attributes.

Participate in elaborate interpersonal engagements while maximizing time effectiveness.

Participating in scholarly conversations with peers is stimulating, cultivating an atmosphere of imaginative thinking where invention flourishes. Interacting with individuals hailing from varied industries can result in fresh viewpoints, significant metamorphoses, and important affiliations.

Partake in challenging pursuits and enigmas as a form of recreational activity.

Gaining mastery in a new language or musical instrument fosters the simultaneous activation of both cerebral hemispheres, an attribute that is truly extraordinary. Furthermore, puzzles and brainteasers facilitate the development of both logical and creative cognitive abilities.

Take Time Out

It is crucial that each member of your team places a high priority on allocating regular intervals dedicated to rest and relaxation. I strongly advocate for the implementation of regular breaks within your team, as it has been observed that individuals often rejuvenate their minds and foster a positive outlook upon their return.

Learning To Think Systematically

The comprehension of systematic thinking should not be equated with the comprehension of systems themselves. It entails a comprehension of the origins of the routine challenges encountered by individuals.

Challenges pertaining to problem solving frequently arise due to a lack of recognition that incidents are interconnected rather than occurring in isolation.

Resolving intricate matters necessitates the application of systematic reasoning. Adopting impromptu approaches can result in unanticipated ramifications, potentially exacerbating the problem.

Patterns occur constantly. If we perceive our existence as a narrative, these recurring patterns would be symbolized by repetitive storylines characterized by comparable motifs. These archetypal themes ought to be regarded as indicative of an imminent or necessary shift in behavior.

Seek areas of strategic advantage. Attaining the most favorable outcomes frequently necessitates operating within a prescribed framework or structure, even if it initially appears contrary to intuition.

Acknowledge that the most effective approach to solving most problems involves the simultaneous implementation of various methods and solutions. Disregard the inclination to perceive a problem as having only one solution.

Consider the system as a cohesive unit or entity. Although family members are interconnected by blood ties, they possess distinct individual lives and goals. The actions of family members, despite their strong bond as a group, can occasionally yield unforeseen outcomes. The intricate nature of the dynamics within a system, family, or team is such that they frequently yield unfavorable outcomes.

Devote yourself wholeheartedly to the pursuit of knowledge in order to cultivate the bravery to embrace

mistakes. A high level of expertise is acquired through the careful examination of our own cognitive frameworks and mechanisms.
Cultivate a mindset that prioritizes long-term considerations over short-term impulses, acquiring the necessary knowledge and proactively making the choice to forgo immediate gratification in favor of making enduring investments towards achieving success.

Systematic thinking does not allow for opportunistic thinking which is often a risky and emotional decision. This does not imply that systematic thinkers are devoid of opportunism, rather it signifies that they diligently assess opportunities before proceeding with them.
A significant amount of time is devoted to the examination of individuals' intelligence, thereby constituting a fundamental issue in the realm of education today. Collective or social intelligence does not revolve around the individual who possesses the

highest level of intellect within a given space. A team should be based on the collective intelligence and our potential achievements as a whole.

Improving Your Social Intelligence

What does the term 'social intelligence' entail and how does it hold relevance in your life?

A significant differentiation lies between the individual who attains expertise and the one who approximates it but falls short, and that is the possession of social intelligence—the ability to perceive individuals for who they truly are, rather than simply conforming to our preconceived notions of them.

According to the writings of Robert Greene in his influential work titled Mastery, it is crucial to acknowledge and address the existence of seven formidable truths, often referred to as "deadly" realities, within both ourselves and others.

Envy
Conformism

Rigidity
Self-obsessiveness
Laziness
Flightiness
Passive Aggression

Many of us function with a sense of naivety, assuming that others perceive the world in the same way as we do and consequently anticipate them to behave in alignment with our own actions. In instances where they fail to do so, we experience anger, a sense of betrayal, or a plethora of adverse and self-deprecating reactions to unfulfilled expectations.

A significant portion of Greene's book Mastery, specifically the final third, is dedicated to elucidating the approaches that individuals attaining mastery must acquire when confronted with the darker aspects of human conduct.

The initial phase entails relinquishing our idealistic perspective in handling individuals and the environment, as per Greene's classification of the seven perilous truths which we should anticipate to manifest in varying magnitudes within all individuals we interact with. If we maintain anticipatory awareness of such behavior, we significantly reduce the likelihood of precipitous reactions when confronted with the need to address them... Whether within our own being or in the individuals surrounding us. By utilizing biographical data obtained about notable and notorious individuals, Greene demonstrates how the destiny of whole scientific theories has been shaped by their level of emotional maturation or, conversely, immaturity.

The Master's paramount consideration in engaging with the external environment is to concentrate on her professional endeavors... Articulate her message by demonstrating meticulous efforts to ensure her work is easily comprehensible, by embracing and incorporating feedback and critique, and by recognizing the futility of her work if it remains impenetrable to her colleagues and the broader populace.

Deliberately and adeptly construct a persona. In this realm of diverse ideologies and contradictory verities, individuals yearn for coherence, openness, and a touch of enigma.

Perceiving oneself through the eyes of others is arguably the most challenging attribute presented by Greene for those of us endeavoring to achieve expertise in our respective domains. In order to achieve this, we need to maintain unwavering objectivity, consistently challenge our ego, and display openness to consider all perspectives concerning our actions.

Suffer fools gladly. The time-honored adage appears antiquated and inconsequential within our society, where a significant portion possesses collegiate qualifications and a substantial number have pursued advanced academic endeavors. Furthermore, it ranks as the least influential factor among the four primary foundations essential for attaining social intelligence. However, if you have had any experience in the business industry, regardless of the duration, you are likely aware of the enduring nature of this advice. In the handling of individuals lacking wisdom, it is imperative to embrace the ensuing mindset: they are merely an integral component of existence, akin to inanimate objects such as rocks or furnishings. Each and every one of us possesses aspects of foolishness... It is human nature."

First, work on yourself.
As a leader, your primary responsibility is to foster personal growth within yourself.
This chapter will elucidate the process of embracing a leader's viewpoint. Additionally, we will engage in a comprehensive analysis of your individual perspectives and principles to determine the most suitable leadership styles for your circumstances.

It will require a substantial period to develop into a proficient leader. The schedule will vary among individuals. Certain individuals may advance at a rapid pace, whereas others may necessitate a longer duration to refine their abilities.

Moreover, it should be noted that although one may acquire the essential pillars of effective leadership, continuous personal and professional growth remains imperative. The final chapter will elucidate this matter, as it comprehensively examines leadership as an ongoing responsibility. Having expressed this, let us proceed with the endeavor of nurturing your leadership potential.

Cultivate a mindset befitting a leader.

It is imperative for a leader to possess a mentality oriented towards continual progress and development. Furthermore, they hold the view that it is imperative for it to foster a distinctive set of beliefs, perspectives, and anticipations. Possessing the appropriate mindset is imperative for one to fulfill the role of a competent leader.

An essential responsibility of a leader entails nurturing the subsequent attributes. "Now, let us proceed to examine the aspects or characteristics they possess:

One often encounters challenges.

As a leader, it is imperative to exhibit courage in the midst of challenging circumstances. Opting to move swiftly towards the tempest is more favorable than choosing to retreat from it. Acknowledge that encountering obstacles will be customary and that you will confront them more often than not.

It is imperative that you establish a well-defined plan for managing such occurrences. You possess an optimistic outlook, anticipating its acceptance and triumph. You will be provided with competent personnel who will offer their assistance whenever required.

Be humble

Even if you are confident in your talents as a leader, it is beneficial to be humble. You intend to acknowledge deserving individuals for their contributions. It would not be prudent to assert sole responsibility and harbor a superiority complex.

Furthermore, it is imperative to embrace the notion that in the event of being proven incorrect, one must take full responsibility and acknowledge it. It is highly undesirable to assign blame to any particular individual. Assuming responsibility for one's actions can yield significant progress.

You display a firm resolve.

A leader should not exhibit any signs of indecisiveness. Particularly when there is limited time available and an immediate decision must be made instead of delaying it. In matters of decisiveness, there must be absolute certainty, without any space for hesitation.

The greater your level of knowledge, the more well-informed your decision-making will be. If acquiring the information would aid you in making a decision, it is advisable to acquire it promptly. Individuals will seek guidance from a leader who exhibits unwavering resolve, particularly when faced with limited time.

Being inventive
Every leader is required to possess resourcefulness. It enhances individuals' capacity to effectively seek solutions amidst challenges. They demonstrate a high level of creativity and exhibit the ability to think innovatively.

They will have an extensive repository of knowledge at their disposal to aid them in addressing inquiries. It will prove advantageous when they encounter their individual challenges. In the event that their team encounters an obstacle, a leader will possess the assurance to provide assistance in surmounting it by virtue of their ingenuity.

Strategizing for the future

Leaders will have the opportunity to proactively strategize. They are contemplating future prospects. They possess an understanding and cognizance of the potential for circumstances to alter.

Upon the occurrence of change, it is imperative for a leader to be well-equipped to undertake suitable adaptations. A growth mindset is apt to be flexible and open to making spontaneous adjustments. In contrast, a steadfast disposition.

A growth mindset anticipates the future and engages in proactive planning. A rigid mindset fails to engage in proactive planning and navigates with a blind optimism, praying to avoid inevitable pitfalls.

Exemplifying honesty and candor.

A true leader must be honest and have nothing to conceal. It is imperative to maintain honesty and transparency with the individuals assisting you in achieving the objectives established for your organization. You seek to apprise them of forthcoming events.

If any alterations are to be made, please inform them in advance. When responding to inquiries, strive to exhibit utmost integrity and credibility. Upon the revelation of your falsehoods, individuals are prone to losing faith in your integrity and may choose to disassociate themselves from you.

The most commendable approach is consistently displaying honesty. It requires a capable leader to make every effort to adhere to it.

Acknowledging the achievements of others

A leader should acknowledge and extend congratulations to individuals who have accomplished success in their own unique manner. They are aware that their efforts have led to the accomplishment of a goal or the successful overcoming of an obstacle. It brought them closer to attaining a noteworthy objective, such as achieving annual sales.

Leaders possess inherent success. Nonetheless, they will yield to their subordinates and acknowledge the credit they duly deserve. Alternatively, they may also bestow commendation upon them for their exemplary performance.

Taking on responsibility

You shall bear the responsibility in the event of any unfortunate occurrences. Do not assign blame to others. It is imperative to formulate a solution to rectify any potential deviations from what is morally or ethically acceptable, if deemed necessary.

People make errors. Leaders such as yourself are not an assemblage of machinery, but rather individuals of human nature. Despite your personal conviction, there will inevitably arise instances where your assumptions prove to be erroneous.

What type of leader do you perceive yourself to be?

Within this section, we shall delve into the discussion surrounding the most suitable leadership style that aligns with your individual characteristics and needs. We will examine the fundamental attributes exhibited by leaders of these categories, enabling you to discern the alignment of your personal beliefs and principles. "Allow us to examine the various styles listed below:

Autocratic

This particular category of leader upholds the principle of absolute authority and adherence to their decisions. Their pronouncements are considered definitive and non-negotiable. They will exhibit a diminished willingness to embrace novel concepts, discussions, or any other form of input. Consequently, the contribution of a team member may go unnoticed.

They implement policies without prior notice. This can prove to be advantageous when applied within limited groups or sectors such as the armed forces or governmental organizations. This could be deemed unsuitable in virtually all commercial scenarios.

Democratic

Whilst you will possess authority pertaining to the daily functioning, a significant proportion of decision-making will involve the active participation of your team. Indeed, this approach would prove ineffective in urgent situations (where a slightly authoritarian approach may be permissible). In addition to that, this will facilitate a platform for your team members to engage in the exchange of their thoughts and ideas.

They are also capable of assisting you in making crucial business determinations. After the presentation of all ideas, the prevailing consensus will determine the selection of the most favorable alternative. Subsequently, it is implemented.

Transformational

An exemplary category would be that of a transformational leader. This is attributable to their ability to enhance the capabilities of their workforce.

Moreover, they possess a visionary mindset, brimming with unique insights, and are driven by an unwavering desire to seamlessly translate their ideas into tangible reality.

This can be utilized in conjunction with particular leadership methodologies, particularly in instances where the objective is to foster beneficial transformative outcomes.

Diplomatic

The primary objective of a diplomatic leader is to foster contentment and satisfaction among all parties involved. Occasionally, it may be necessary to engage in negotiations to ensure that the aspirations of all parties involved are met. This is the kind of leader who possesses the capability to rectify any circumstance, regardless of its intricacy.

Bureaucratic

There is an established hierarchy of authority. The highest level of power and control shall be vested in a leader of eminent rank. Beneath the highest level, there will exist additional leaders, each presiding over their own hierarchy of personnel.

This is widespread within the military context, however, it is plausible that an analogous framework may exist within the realm of business. In matters pertaining to the company, the Chief Executive Officer possesses the ultimate decision-making authority. Nevertheless, it is important to note that a subordinate leader is required to provide regular updates to a superior leader (for instance, a branch manager will be subject to the jurisdiction of a regional manager).

Transactional

This category of leader will duly acknowledge and incentivize individuals who perform admirably, while concurrently imposing consequences upon those who exhibit subpar performance. Please regard it as analogous to a physical activity. It is advisable to suspend a star athlete who is experiencing a continued streak of losses until they exhibit noticeable improvement in their performance.

In the event that a prominent athlete demonstrates exceptional performance, regardless of their role as a starter or substitute, they will be granted supplementary playing time as a recognition of their achievements. It holds true within the world of business. Thus, it is important to observe and record individuals who are actively contributing to and those who are impeding the progress of the team.

Maturity as a leader is a gradual process that requires a significant investment of time. Moreover, it will aid you in cultivating and defining your personal leadership ethos. Developing a mindset will prove to be a formidable challenge on your journey of personal growth.
However, you can rest assured that you possess the capability to comprehend the necessary elements for making astute decisions, acknowledging the contributions of your team, and assuming accountability for various matters, including admitting to any

erroneous beliefs or opinions. It is now imperative to proceed and address several paramount responsibilities that you, in your capacity as a leader, must assume.

Who Are You?

comes to mind is typically being in charge and giving orders. However, true leadership goes beyond simply holding authority and involves guiding and inspiring others towards a common goal."

One potential concept that arises is that of control or dominance. Then

Following a direct interaction with a leader, a transformative change may transpire.

From a viewpoint or perspective.

Regardless of the veracity of this statement, it is imperative to take into account

that every individual possesses their distinctive manner of existence leader. position of leadership, others prefer to maintain a more passive role and follow the direction of others."

While certain individuals exhibit a preference for taking a more subdued role, they consistently fulfill their essential responsibilities without falter.

responsibilities.

Regardless of one's character, have it in mind that...

Please be aware that there exists a leadership style that perfectly aligns with your needs.

with your personality. "We exhibit distinct individualities, thus,

Our approach to leadership must differ. Below is an

Examination of diverse individuals' character traits and their suitability for leadership positions.

They have the potential to emerge as:

- The Diligent Leader: This individual with a meticulous nature

fosters the development of leaders who thoroughly analyze particulars, possess a meticulous attention to detail, and demonstrate a strategic mindset

Precise and systematic decision-making approach, based on sound logic

steps. They generally exhibit a subdued demeanor, consequently, reach capacity

space characterized by a strong inclination towards meticulous organization

and to assume responsibility for all aspects. This type of leader place greater importance on adopting a gradual approach.

They are proceeding with caution to guarantee

Exemplary standards of perfection, meticulous precision, and unwavering integrity

their plans. They're very straightforward, thus,

their plans are accessible to all individuals. The meticulous

The individual will ensure that they have meticulously

weighed the pros and cons of

prior to implementation, they discuss and finalize their plans.

The drawback of the fastidious leader is that they

become excessively immersed in rectifying matters,

Frequently, they fail to consider the larger perspective.

They rarely afford others the opportunity to take the lead.

hence, they can be perceived as unfeeling, lacking in diplomacy and etiquette.

unemphathic. • The Resolute Leader: These individuals possess exceptional determination and fortitude.

leaders. They derive satisfaction from asserting their dominance and being resilient.

Authorities with decision-making power and apprehension surrounding their strict measures

has the potential to facilitate the successful completion of tasks for an entire team

at a faster pace than anticipated. They are very efficient

Moreover, they are renowned for their impartiality and objectivity. Many

At certain moments, it appears as though they desire to take charge of the situation.

everything at once but in actuality, they like

Collaborating with individuals and constructing what is commonly acknowledged.

as work relationships. Like the meticulous leader,

Additionally, they devise strategies to accomplish tasks with lucidity.

Upon careful evaluation of the advantages and disadvantages...

However, one must acknowledge the drawback of assuming such a leadership role...

They exhibit a disregard for the emotions of others and fail to show respect.

exhibit suboptimal abilities in managing individuals. They are barely

Given their open-minded nature, they become excessively self-absorbed, rendering them oblivious to the ramifications of their choices.

every other person. However, they sometimes

derive pleasure from collaborating and engaging in productive work sessions with

individuals possessing exceptional cognitive abilities and displaying sound judgment, similar to their traits.

- The Considerate Leader: The considerate leader

can potentially be perceived as hostile and excessively

serious'. "They exhibit unwavering dedication and

dedicated to their assignments; therefore, they ensure to

Ensure that all details are carefully attended to and every aspect is thoroughly addressed.

They exhibit a high level of meticulousness and systematicity, to the point of being almost fastidious.

Excessively diligent, yet be mindful to uphold

Collaboration among the subordinate teams. They

are precise and concise, focusing on particular details

We anticipate that their requirements will be fully fulfilled.

way they require. They carefully contemplate the impact of their decisions on individuals, taking into consideration their concerns and well-being.

they make them.

The conscientious leader may encounter a difficulty with.

Determining the significance of goals and prioritizing them

are not. They have an aversion to confrontations, therefore

They might be uncapable of reaching any decision.

will affect anyone. It is recommended/encouraged/advised/prudent to pursue this type of

It is imperative for a leader to possess a team of proficient advisors who can provide assistance and guidance.

manage strategies.

- The Benevolent Leader: if you possess this type of disposition

If you consistently demonstrate dedicated efforts and persistent commitment to your role as a leader,

Positively impactful on the morale and motivation of your team members. They are the

Encouragers, who engage in interpersonal interactions, demonstrate emotional sensitivity.

and ensure that all individuals are content with the

condition of the professional environment. provides guidance to others."

Occasionally, individuals exert significant efforts to contribute to the success of their team.

I am at ease with the possibility that they may go unnoticed in the role of

voice of authority. However, deep within their

In addition to displaying benevolence, they also guarantee the prompt completion of tasks.

with fervor and dynamism.

In spite of the benevolence displayed by the magnanimous leader...

They might display a great degree of subjectivity in their decision.

making process. "They consistently aim to satisfy others and as a result,

may fail to achieve the company's objectives

and visions a priority as long as it affect the

team's harmony. They are unable to achieve a state of equilibrium in terms of logical reasoning.

and the aspect of their being that pertains to emotions. For a leader

In this manner, having the guidance of an advisor would be highly advantageous. • The Strategic Leader: These individuals possess a pragmatic mindset.

They demonstrate high levels of effectiveness and efficiency in their performance.

Individuals primarily assume roles due to their limited allocation of energy

transforming them into viable and attainable strategies

opportunities and tactics. They allow

fostering of independent thought and promotion of

concept of individualism. The tactical leader is

Amenable to the consideration of diverse opinions and perspectives.

separated themselves from the rest of the team and granted permission to all individuals

engage in the self-exploration of their own methods for achieving

success. Nevertheless, as attentively as they may heed

People and promote autonomy, they also enjoy

work alone.

One of the drawbacks of assuming the role of a strategic leader is that

They lack the capability to anticipate long-term outcomes.

Individuals possess the ability to function effectively in solitude and exhibit discomfort when their personal boundaries are encroached upon, thus potentially hindering collaboration.

Regarded as an individual who excels in interpersonal skills and communication with others. To excel in leadership,

They must cultivate and enhance their intuitive faculties.

Place greater emphasis on elucidating a strategic foresight

for the organization.

- The empathetic leaders: These individuals demonstrate compassion through their actions and decisions.

The leaders who exhibit activist tendencies. They are gentle,

Possesses empathy and a deep understanding of the human experience.

circumstances and hold the conviction that all individuals possess certain factors

right that mandates complete reverence. They're all

for endorsing the individual widely regarded as

supporting a disadvantaged entity and channeling their efforts towards

Champion and advocate for the disadvantaged. Thus,

They possess unwavering determination, firm decisiveness, and keen consciousness.

they frequently contemplate the consequences of their actions and

Decisions contribute to the betterment of others. One drawback of this particular leadership style is that it is deemed as (or perceived to be) difficult to tolerate.

challenging to acclimate to strictness. They are flexible, hence,

They do not have a preference for being continuously connected to one thing.

I have been involved in this project for an extended period. They are so

Show empathy by allowing them to catch the bus

the entire team, as a result of their reluctance to terminate any individuals

That is not in accordance with established standards or guidelines. Acquiring the services of an executive aide.

It is highly recommended to opt for a more strategic and formidable approach.

- The Resourceful Leader: These individuals embody the qualities of an enterprising leader.

characterized by a strong emphasis on competition and innovation. Every

Each day, individuals embrace novel opportunities and embark upon fresh endeavors.

novel avenues of expansion for their own enterprises and

pertaining to the organization under their direction. Above this, they

They are open to undertaking numerous experiments, leading to a willingness to take risks.

individuals who possess an insatiable desire for

Engaging in experimentation of novel endeavors. They possess great strategic acumen and possess an extensive knowledge regarding...

Addressing challenges and circumventing potential setbacks. The

An innovative and proactive leader adopts a methodical and deliberate approach.

Towards opportunities they explore.

analyze the opportunities, evaluate their advantages and disadvantages, and

Subsequently, formulate the optimal approach to tackle the aforementioned issue.

Incomplete initiatives have become customary for these esteemed leaders.

as they become enthralled by the arrival of a new

project. They frequently exhibit a tendency to delay or postpone tasks.

notwithstanding their high level of competitiveness,

They possess a multitude of alternative options. Owing to their contingency plans,

Due to their competitive disposition, they can be rather offensive.

examining alternative viewpoints due to

They prioritize their own values and ideas over those of others.

everyone else. • The Forward-thinking Leader: These individuals possess exceptional perception and foresight

and perceptive individuals who consistently possess a strong desire to "work towards the preservation of the human race" and by the means of their verbal expressions and actions

actions successfully attend to the needs of all individuals

team. they strive for excellence and meticulously ensure that"

Their approach is devoid of any mistakes or errors.

corporate operations and deliberation procedures. The

A visionary leader expects a great deal from his or her subordinates.

the individuals themselves, as well as all of their employees

there is consistently an objective within reach, or a groundbreaking methodology for accomplishing a particular task. The determination made by an individual with foresight

The leader's reliance on the future is profound, and

How the course of events will unfold and impact all individuals.

They exhibit a strong dedication to work, hence their consistent conscientiousness

propensity for comprehending individuals in their entirety. They attempt to

Striving for perfection, an unattainable goal, can result in exhausting oneself in the pursuit. They

may encounter difficulties in being direct, possess a strong inclination

The aforementioned viewpoint is subjective and may give rise to the identification of potential strategies for resolving conflicts.

difficult.

they do best and trust them to complete their tasks independently."

'they desire' serves as the guiding principle of this style of leadership.

In this particular scenario, the leader delegates full authority to

their team to implement all the requisite measures andactions

decisions without any form of intervention. The leader

equips their team with extensive expertise and ingenuity

liberty, wisdom, and requisite adaptability

In order to facilitate their management of the matter.

things.

One disadvantage of this approach is that it has the potential to place

The team leader's position faces considerable risk if the appropriate tasks are not assigned to suitable individuals, and the leader

shall be required to assume responsibility for any implications that may arise from their actions

happens.

As emphasized earlier, note that the same leadership

The style may not be universally suitable for all situations and individuals. It

It is imperative to acknowledge that both a team and its leader have the capacity to attempt.

Explore various leadership approaches and adhere to those that are most effective.

that are effective in their case. It should be mentioned that in a

With regards to a specific leader, a subset of leadership approaches may

There may be instances of convergence where overlap occurs, prompting leaders to occasionally adopt varied leadership approaches tailored to specific circumstances and cohorts.

The Confident Leader

Confidence can be defined as the unwavering belief in oneself and one's capabilities. Do not indulge in the contemplation of doubt and inquiry regarding your adequacy, resilience, or valor. This becomes particularly noticeable in situations that necessitate a display of audaciousness.

The self-assured leader is an individual who possesses the readiness to assume challenging responsibilities with a positive mindset. Individuals desire to be guided by an individual who possesses the attributes of composure, attentiveness, and unwavering determination, all of which cannot be attained without a substantiated level of self-assurance.

In addition, the unwavering self-assurance exhibited by such a leader can prove to be infectious, instilling a sense of belief and self-assurance within the entire team. Adversities and challenges are inherent in all endeavors, however, should the team leader demonstrate a lack of assurance in surmounting them, the cohesion and effectiveness of the entire team would be compromised.

How to Become One:

Confidence is not an attribute that emerges instantaneously; rather, it requires consistent daily cultivation to foster its growth. "In order to establish oneself as a confident leader, it is advisable to implement the following strategies:

Be a planner. It is inherent to human nature to experience a sensation of assurance when an event or outcome can be foreseen. Developing a comprehensive strategy with tangible measures will facilitate the realization that progress is achievable, thereby enhancing your self-assurance. In addition, enhanced forecasting of potential obstacles can be facilitated by meticulously outlining each step required to progress towards the desired objective. In the event of unforeseen and surprising circumstances, effective planning proves invaluable, as a competent leader must invariably possess contingency measures.

Acquire proficiency in the practice of power dressing. An individual's capacity to appear well-groomed unavoidably impacts their sense of self-assurance. Do you not concur that it is considerably simpler to place trust in an individual who presents themselves in a well-groomed manner? To emerge as a self-assured leader, it is imperative to project a suitable appearance. Naturally, it is not suggested that one should deplete their financial resources solely to acquire a costly suit, though it must be emphasized that the acquisition of such an attire is an investment that aligns with the values upheld by esteemed leaders. You can initiate the process by dedicating an additional five minutes per day to guaranteeing that your garments exhibit a well-pressed and flattering appearance, you emit a pleasant scent, and your hairstyle is impeccable.

Give careful consideration to nonverbal cues. Do you ensure that you maintain a straight posture, with your shoulders retracted and your chest extended? Are you consistently exhibiting an open posture during your interactions, or do you frequently adopt a closed stance by crossing your arms and lowering your head? Exemplary leaders are individuals who exude self-assurance and conduct themselves with poise and sophistication. If one perceives a deficiency in this realm, it is advisable to consistently endeavor to rectify one's bodily posture and cultivate enhanced awareness of their handshaking technique and overall presentation, particularly in gestures and demeanor when interacting with others.

One paramount recommendation that can be offered with regard to fostering confidence is to unequivocally have faith in oneself. Upon rising every morning, affirm "I possess strength and unwavering self-assurance." When an individual has unwavering faith in their own abilities, it often elicits confidence and trust from others.

Non-Verbal Communication Can Facilitate Interpersonal Interactions.

In addition to acquiring verbal communication skills, it is imperative to recognize the significance of non-verbal communication. By adopting this approach, you can facilitate mutual understanding among individuals while also ensuring that you effectively fulfill the duties of an efficient leader.

As it is often said, deeds hold more weight than mere words. It is crucial for you to possess the awareness and ability to discern the emotions of individuals in your vicinity through non-verbal communication. Develop the ability to interpret and discern their nonverbal cues, such as their facial expressions or body language. An exemplary leader and a proficient communicator is an individual who possesses the capacity to adeptly employ signs and symbols, requiring no explicit elucidation through verbal means to comprehend the situation.

If one possesses adept proficiency in non-verbal communication, the following outcomes can ensue:

Repetition. They have the capability to disseminate the information you have just conveyed, thereby ensuring a wide-reaching transmission of the message to a significant audience.

Complimenting. Individuals may offer praise for your adeptness in effectively conveying information and may express admiration for your appearance or manner of speech.

In the interim, in the event that one lacks proficiency in non-verbal communication, substitution may occur. This is an instance in which individuals may express erroneous statements or convey a disparate message to others due to a lack of comprehension regarding your intended communication. Exercise caution in both your speech and behavior.

The enumerated classifications of Non-Verbal Communication are as delineated below:

Proximity. This represents the spatial separation between oneself and the individual with whom conversation is taking place. Certainly, if one seeks to facilitate the successful negotiation of a deal or attract someone's attention, it would be advisable to maintain proximity to the individual in question. It is important, however, to exercise caution and avoid invading personal space to such an extent that it becomes discomforting, particularly in instances where there is a difference in gender between the parties involved. Direct your undivided attention towards the individual. By following this approach, you will undoubtedly achieve excellent outcomes.

Posture and Body Language. Examples of nonverbal communication include the act of crossing one's arms, making deliberate hair movements, or placing a hand on one's waist. Expressions of attitudes and emotions can be communicated through these aforementioned movements, as well as through one's bodily posture. Having proper posture increases the likelihood of being regarded with admiration, as opposed to appearing uncertain or lacking confidence due to slouching or a lack of self-assurance. Your stance and body language convey valuable insights into your character and undoubtedly impact your standing among others.

Para-linguistics. This pertains to an individual's vocal tone, pitch, and modulation. The manner in which you articulate your thoughts will invariably be analyzed, hence it is imperative to refrain from immediate response and rather invest contemplation into the execution of your words. Occasionally, despite possessing genuine intentions, an inadequate proficiency in articulation can hinder one's ability to effectively communicate, resulting in limited receptivity from others. An effective leader possesses the ability to capture individuals' attention and command their listening. One methodology for achieving this is to ensure the precision and finesse of one's verbal delivery.

Gestures. Nonverbal cues can accurately convey an individual's emotions and intentions, rendering the need for verbal communication unnecessary. Illustrations of gestures comprise actions such as indicating, gesturing, or employing one's digits for enumeration or demonstration of another person's actions. It would be advantageous to gain further knowledge about the diverse gestures exhibited by individuals from various cultural backgrounds.

Facial Expressions. It is evident that only an individual lacking sensitivity would be unable to discern an individual's contentment or dissatisfaction with their activities based on their facial expressions of either frowning or smiling. One can discern various emotions such as joy, irony, rage, desolation, vexation, and essentially an array of feelings by observing an individual's facial expressions.

Eye Gazing. According to commonly held belief, if one is unable to establish direct eye contact, it is indicative of potential dishonesty. Although this may not hold universally, it is generally more preferable to maintain eye contact while engaging in conversation with someone. This demonstrates a genuine effort on your part to capture their attention, emphasize their importance, and indicate your unwavering commitment to the subject matter at hand. Gaze into someone's eyes and promptly command their undivided attention.

Appearance. It is crucial to note that one's manner of self-presentation carries significant importance when interacting with others. One's hairstyle, choice of attire, and application of cosmetic products can convey significant insights into one's character or the persona one aims to present. As an individual in a leadership position, maintaining a polished appearance and avoiding any appearance of carelessness is of utmost significance. It is equally crucial that one avoids using an insufficient or excessive amount of cosmetics. Exemplify qualities that command admiration and respect, and rest assured that others will be attentively receptive to your words.

It is important to bear in mind that effective leadership entails the aptitude to communicate with others in a distinctly articulate manner. If one possesses the ability to engage in verbal communication, it is expected that they would also possess the ability to engage in non-verbal communication.

Management Skills

Leadership begins with management. An organization characterized by a well-structured, composed, and serene environment serves as an indication of effective governance. Management entails the effective allocation and utilization of available resources within the organizational setting. This encompasses, primarily, the workforce responsible for executing the designated responsibilities, along with the tangible assets required for the workforce to fulfill these obligations.

Human capital encompasses the cadre of personnel comprising the organization, arranged in a pecking order according to their competencies, educational attainment, and vocational track record. Physical capital pertains to the infrastructure and associated amenities within a work environment, encompassing devices such as computers, furnishings like tables and chairs, supplies such as stationery, utilities such as water and lighting, and climate control systems such as air-conditioning.

Efficient management ought to ensure that both the aforementioned resources of labor and physical capital operate at their maximum capacity, thereby minimizing any instances of waste. An illustrative instance of the efficient utilization of physical resources is the implementation of a paper recycling initiative. Rather than printing every document on a single sheet, adopting the practice of printing documents on both sides can be employed. Additionally, in the context of documents being submitted for examination during a meeting with the intention of discarding them afterwards, it is possible to utilize the reverse side of already printed single-sided paper for printing purposes. The cost savings resulting from this approach, encompassing both the financial impact on the organization and the environmental implications for society, will prove to be significant.

Managing physical resources is relatively straightforward, whereas effectively overseeing human resources presents a managerial challenge. Now, let us delve into the topics pertaining to management and personnel within the section dedicated to enhancing management abilities.

Identifying Skill Sets

The optimal candidate for the appropriate position.

A demonstration of the optimal allocation of staff resources involves the strategic assignment of personnel that aligns their skills with the corresponding role. In typically circumstances, individuals are recruited by a company following a thorough interview process, subsequently being assigned to the department with an available position that was the subject of an advertised vacancy, to which the applicant in question applied.

During the early stages of her employment, Nicole exhibits exemplary performance in carrying out her designated responsibilities and showcases her expertise in client communication via telephone. Everyone is happy.

However, the manager possesses a discerning observation skills, as he discerns that Nicole's abilities extend beyond effectively communicating with individuals over the phone, which is the primary duty she was originally employed for. In addition to her aptitude for verbal communication, he recognizes that she also possesses exceptional writing skills. This discovery was made while Nicole was prompted to present a written document outlining her interactions with clients. Her proficiency in written work is an aptitude that had eluded detection by others. Therefore, the manager initiates a conversation with Nicole whereby he inquires whether she would be willing to undertake the task of composing project reports for the organization. Nicola is highly enthusiastic about utilizing her writing abilities in a professional capacity. The manager has implemented a 50% reduction in the amount of time allocated for phone communication, and has subsequently allocated the remaining portion for the task of composing project reports.

As a consequence, the manager has successfully discerned the most suitable candidate for the respective role, thereby instilling a sense of fulfillment in the staff member as well.

A prevalent observation regarding the work habits of employees is that, typically after a duration of two or three years in their current position, they develop a feeling of monotony associated with their job role. They persist in this endeavor either due to a lack of ambition to alter their path or because the monetary compensation is satisfactory enough to dissuade their desire to leave. Effective managerial skills encompass the capacity to remain vigilant towards employee disengagement and discern their untapped abilities that can be applied in various domains within the corporate setting. Consequently, the company stands to gain by avoiding any extra expenses while simultaneously ensuring employee satisfaction, as the repetitiveness of their roles is alleviated through engagement in novel tasks.

Another recurring observation regarding the staff is that they are assigned tasks that either do not align with their preferences or fall outside their areas of expertise. An employee who lacks the necessary interpersonal skills may not find a front office reception job to be suitable, as an illustration. An employee of this nature may experience a depletion of internal energy as a result of engaging in continuous interactions with others throughout the day. A skilled manager will recognize this characteristic, and instead of reprimanding the employee for her insufficient interpersonal abilities, will privately approach her and ascertain her strengths. He is capable of allocating to her a task that matches her skill level; additionally, he can allocate another individual who possesses proficient social skills. Throughout the course of the endeavor, all parties involved experience contentment.

Therefore, a fundamental competency in management involves the ability to discern the most suitable individual for a given role. In the role of a manager, you possess the ability to cultivate a comprehensive inventory of employee competencies and facilitate the rotation of individuals across various departments within the organizational framework, taking into consideration these skill profiles. The introduction of this shift in pace and nature of work is likely to be favorably received by the majority of employees, who view it as a valuable opportunity facilitated by the company to enhance their professional development. There may be certain employees who exhibit resistance towards embracing change; in such cases, it is preferable to refrain from disturbing their mindset, as the saying goes - "you can lead a horse to water, but you cannot make it drink."

Delegation of Labor

Macro-management.

For numerous leaders, the prospect of delegating assignments to their subordinates can instill fear. Leaders of this nature endure restless nights contemplating the potential shortcomings of their staff in fulfilling their duties. Moreover, they harbor concerns regarding the timeliness of the staff's completion of the assignment. Consequently, they embark on incessantly contacting the staff via email or phone, demanding regular updates regarding the progress of the task. Certain managers go as far as expressing a genuine interest in determining which staff members will undertake the responsibility of ushering participants at the forthcoming conference, as well as identifying those who will be tasked with distributing the name tags. Colleagues in managerial positions instruct employees regarding appropriate conduct when in the company of the chairman.

This type of executive is recognized as a "micromanaging" individual, someone who seeks to maintain a high level of control over the intricate details of tasks. The staff typically harbors strong antipathy towards a micro-manager.

Why so? The fundamental aspect of micromanagement lies in the manager's lack of confidence in her staff's capability to carry out the designated assignments diligently and meet the specified deadline. All personnel are cognizant of their work obligations, and strongly resent incessant reminders regarding the execution of said obligations. Additionally, the incessant prompting and requests for progress updates from the supervisor not only fail to guarantee the employee's focus on their tasks, but rather serve as a source of annoyance, consequently posing a significant diversion from the immediate work responsibilities. The employee is constantly apprehensive that he may be summoned at any given time to deliver progress reports on the tasks he has been assigned.

Micro-management can also arise from a manager's inclination to retain complete dominion over the entire process. He holds the belief that relinquishing authority over the staff's approach to the task will result in the erosion of his control.

When employees perceive that their level of accountability is being scrutinized and that their level of trust in the manager is diminished, they tend to foster feelings of inferiority and harboring personal antipathy towards the manager. That is an unfavorable situation with potential to initiate a cascade of diminishing employee morale, ultimately permeating the entire company.

A leader of this caliber must acquire proficiency in the art of macro-level management. A leader ought to prioritize the overarching vision of accomplishing the company's goals and objectives, rather than getting engrossed in insignificant particulars pertaining to the execution of the task. The responsibility falls upon a junior supervisor or a section head, who diligently monitors the project's progress in real-time, providing timely feedback to the manager during scheduled events such as staff meetings or section heads' meetings. A competent manager ought to grant their employees the essential liberty to think and act in manners that empower them to effectively execute their assigned tasks.

Macro-management entails instilling trust in the employees and having faith in the operational procedures.

The Importance Of Interpersonal Connections And Proficient Verbal And Non-Verbal Exchange

In order to exemplify effective leadership, it is crucial for individuals to possess a comprehensive comprehension of the true essence of communication. There is a prevailing belief held by certain individuals that a leader must incessantly monopolize the conversation, yet a significant number of the esteemed leaders in history would vehemently contest this notion. Effective communicators are the hallmark of competent leaders. They possess the ability to effectively convey their messages and possess a magnetic charm that effortlessly captivates the attention of others.

First Key Quality - Demonstrates Active Listening

Individuals have the capacity to perceive sound, yet not every individual actively processes or comprehends auditory input. Frequently, during conversations, our tendency is to merely listen without truly comprehending. Effective leaders possess the trait of not only engaging in active listening, but also demonstrating a high level of attentiveness while doing so. They consistently ensure that the speaker's voice is acknowledged and that viewpoints are articulated. Leaders who have achieved success in leading a team of one hundred individuals can affirm that possessing excellent listening skills is a vital trait for effective leadership. It entails maintaining silence and attentively listening to the perspectives and opinions of one's constituents.

It is essential to consider that ideas should not solely originate from your own perspective, as each member of your team possesses valuable contributions to offer. If you persist in regarding your opinion or idea as infallible, I implore you to reconsider. Adopting such a mindset would pave the path towards inevitable failure. A competent leader is attentive and receptive to the thoughts and opinions of their followers.

Second Key Attribute - Demonstrates Effective Communication Skills

It is possible to exhibit traits of authority and confidence while maintaining a respectful regard for the viewpoints of others. A proficient leader should acquire the skill of effectively declining requests or offers without causing hurt or offense. There is no necessity to exhibit rudeness in order to assert dominance or attract attention from one's supporters. Effective diction, quality substance, and a composed demeanor invariably captivate the attention of the listeners. It is imperative to bear in mind the discourse required by one's audience. Nonetheless, it is imperative to refrain from diluting your words in an attempt to cater to the sentiments of your audience. Ensure that honesty and credibility are maintained while expressing oneself.

Always remember the fundamental nature of the information you are communicating, so as to effectively convey the message to your audience. One additional aspect that you should bear in mind is the importance of deliberating beforehand on the subject matter you wish to address. Please contemplate thoroughly prior to verbalizing any statements. Additionally, it is imperative for a leader to possess the capability to communicate effectively and concisely with their subordinates. Speak with assuredness to ensure that your communication is not dismissed. Please address your statements with due consideration towards your audience. It is imperative to bear in mind that individuals will retain the manner in which you articulate your thoughts; hence, it is crucial to convey your ideas with utmost clarity. Condense your message and maintain a direct approach. Carefully consider your audience to determine the appropriate information to communicate to them.

Thirdly, one should actively solicit a response.

It is advisable to consistently seek the input or perspectives of others regarding the matter at hand. Request feedback and remain receptive to the emotions expressed by your followers. Effective leaders have a strong inclination towards acquiring knowledge and insights from those they lead. The intention behind this is simply to convey to your followers that their opinions are highly regarded and they are encouraged to freely express their thoughts on a specific subject matter. Please ensure that your team comprehends that the objective of communication is to generate an idea or prompt a call to action. By according due importance to their opinions, ideas, and expressions, you will effectively cultivate long-lasting relationships with them. All individuals desire to express themselves, including those who choose to follow you.

Quality #4 – Adhere to veracity

It is ineffective to employ euphemisms when communicating with one's constituents. In addition to the time inefficiency, circumventing the issue reflects incompetence and a dearth of assurance. At present, there is no immediate requirement for these. Therefore, it is advisable to always communicate with clarity and honesty.

The Impact Of Leadership Styles" Or "The Consequences Of Different Leadership Approaches

Leadership style refers to the conduct demonstrated by a leader in the guidance and oversight of individuals under their supervision. The manner in which he conducts himself and interacts with his subordinates influences their behavior, thus determining the overall style observed.

Whilst a leader has the ability to exert their authority in various manners, it is crucial to acknowledge that the style employed ultimately dictates the level of motivation, efficiency, and effectiveness exhibited by their subordinates. Despite the fact that there are numerous leadership styles that vary among different leaders, the four primary styles include:

a) Authoritarian Approach - This approach encompasses the utilization of coercive tactics and intimidation by the manager to ensure that subordinates complete assigned tasks. There is substantial utilization of coercive measures in the execution of tasks.

b) The Autocratic Styles - Within this management approach, decision-making authority is concentrated in the hands of the leader, while the involvement and participation of subordinates are actively discouraged. It exhibits a 'tell-style' approach characterized by unilateral communication. The leader provides instructions to subordinates without providing them with the rationale behind those instructions. This approach suppresses the initiatives of subordinates and diminishes their morale and dedication to their work.

Within a media organization, the editor, alongside other managerial personnel, employs a particular approach when deliberating upon and subsequently communicating decisions. They offer subordinates the opportunity to provide input by presenting their decisions, but they may ultimately choose not to incorporate the feedback received. Many organizations tend to embrace the benevolent form of leadership, wherein the editor establishes policies and disregards input from subordinates based on the belief that the decision is in the best interest of the organization. Nevertheless, an authentic autocratic approach persists within any organization controlled by an individual who, for the most part, anticipates that tasks be executed in accordance with their own preferences. The manager's decision to adopt an autocratic leadership style could possibly stem from the perception that subordinates lack proficiency and motivation. An advantage of this approach is that tasks are completed within the specified timeframes, as seeking input from colleagues does not pose an obstacle.

c) The Democratic (Participatory) style - In contrast to the autocratic style, decision-making is decentralized in nature. It is alternatively referred to as the 'join style'. The leader assigns responsibilities to subordinates based on their competence and interest. The effectiveness of this delegation relies on their willingness to actively engage. Managers who employ this approach propose rough concepts and solicit input, or present a challenge and seek ideas to facilitate the refinement of their own stance.

The benefits of this approach include enhancing employees' sense of self-esteem and contentment, fostering a sense of self-realization through active involvement in decision-making, potentially improving the quality of decision-making through employee input, and facilitating smoother implementation of changes due to the input provided by subordinates.

The 'abdicratic' leadership style, also known as the laissez-faire or 'free rein' style, involves the leader relinquishing their leadership responsibilities by assigning them to others. From a technical standpoint, it can be argued that it does not truly qualify as a leadership style; rather, it can be perceived as the absence of one. This interpretation reflects a situation where subordinates are provided with minimal or no guidance, thus being granted the freedom to set their own goals and take full ownership of decision-making processes.

A leader might embrace the 'abdicratic style' as a result of insufficient self-assurance, apprehension towards underperforming, and subjective assessment of the drawbacks associated with leading, which could surpass the benefits.

Managers may choose to embrace this approach if they are convinced that granting their subordinates more autonomy will contribute to improved job performance. Furthermore, it could potentially serve as a more advantageous alternative in situations where the individuals working under authority possess a high level of motivation, extensive expertise, and a demonstrated capability in their respective roles. Under those circumstances, the manager will present a predicament and request them to devise a solution according to their discretion within defined boundaries.

The Leader And Motives

Mark's heart raced with anticipation as he faced his Bishop across the desk. He found it incredulous to perceive the sounds that reached his ears. The Bishop proceeded, expressing his desire for you to establish a church in the neighboring province. "If it proves to be successful, you will have the opportunity to provide strong financial support for your family and enjoy a lifestyle similar to mine." This was the moment he had been anticipating. Finally, he would garner admiration and experience a life of comfort.

Pastor Mark worked hard. He devoted himself incessantly to his modest congregation, serving tirelessly both during the day and throughout the night. Through his resolute guidance, the church experienced substantial growth and achieved prosperity. He commanded the respect of others by virtue of his diligent exertions and esteemed standing within the community. As he strolled along the thoroughfare, individuals consistently extended their greetings, "Greetings, Pastor!" However, following a span of two years marked by accomplishments, a contentious situation transpired between Pastor Mark and the members of his council of elders. The clergyman believed that, in light of his prolonged period of selfless dedication, it would be appropriate for the church to provide him with a spacious residence and a vehicle. The older generation held the belief that his demands were excessive. The matter escalated rapidly, resulting in a subsequent division within the church.

While it is evident that a multitude of factors contributed to the difficulties at hand, it is essential to acknowledge that

Pastor Mark's intentions played a pivotal role in fostering the schism within the church. As the church thrived, Pastor Mark's motivations for assuming leadership became increasingly less admirable, straying significantly from the divine expectations set for those in positions of authority within the church.

This depiction prompts a substantial inquiry that warrants contemplation by leaders in assessing their own worth. What is the driving force behind your leadership aspirations? Can it be attributed to the enjoyment derived from being in a leadership position? Do you actively pursue accolades and endorsement from others? Do you hold the position of a business leader or educator by virtue of divine calling or for personal advancement? This inquiry pertains to the underlying intentions driving your actions. In the context of Christian leadership, the significance of your motives is often on par with the tangible contributions you make. While it is true that a sizable number of leaders possess noble intentions, there are those, such as Mark, who assume positions of leadership driven by ulterior motives. Peter, being a seasoned leader, meticulously crafted guidelines for ecclesiastical authorities that continue to hold significant relevance in the present day and that can aid you in scrutinizing the underlying motivations driving your own leadership endeavors.

I respectfully address the esteemed members of your congregation, humbly beseeching you as a fellow member of the clergy, a testamentary observer of the tribulations endured by Christ, and as one who will partake in the forthcoming revelation of glory. Assume the role of caretakers for the flock bestowed upon you by God, exerting oversight - not out of obligation, but out of willingness as directed by God's desires; not driven by monetary greed, but motivated by a genuine desire to serve; not exercising dominance over those placed in your trust, but demonstrating through your conduct a model for others in the flock. And upon the arrival of the Chief Shepherd, you shall be bestowed with the eternal crown of glory, a token that shall never diminish (1 Peter 5:1-4).

This excerpt is replete with discerning observations catered towards Christian leaders. In the upcoming chapter, my primary emphasis will be directed towards the four motives that Peter has elucidated for Christian leadership.

The leader's intention is genuine

Peter emphasizes the significance of approaching leadership with utmost sincerity. According to his statement, he suggests that individuals ought to engage in service out of their own volition, in alignment with God's desires, rather than out of obligation. Assuming leadership roles entails significant accountability and is unsuitable for those lacking willingness. Christian leadership must never be compelled or prescribed. The validation of your personal calling may frequently be affirmed by others, yet unless it originates from a divine source, you will not achieve success in the realm of Christian leadership. No Christian leader should assume any position in the church, community, or society unless they possess a distinctly discerned divine calling from God.

Calling prevents burnout

In the absence of a distinct vocation or purpose, Christian leadership rapidly transforms into an arduous undertaking. The task of building God's kingdom is perpetual and will remain so until the second coming of Christ. One might exert considerable efforts over a prolonged period of time without witnessing significant outcomes. Frequently, the tangible benefits are limited. Numerous individuals in positions of authority have initiated the endeavor, only to encounter profound weariness of the body, mind, and/or soul. They burned out. Lacking a distinct sense of purpose and a vision propelled by divine inspiration, one's ability to sustain oneself will rapidly diminish.

Calling provides energy

My telephone conversations provide me with the motivation to continue. Although my body may be fatigued, I remain steadfast in my commitment to answer the divine purpose bestowed upon me and persevere without relent. However, this does not imply that I am incapable of taking breaks or pausing momentarily. On the contrary, my sense of purpose reinforces my endurance and propels me to persevere, even under challenging circumstances or when the outcomes are not immediately visible. When I undertake the vocation to which I believe God has summoned me, I find myself invigorated by divine forces. When I am entrusted by the Lord to carry out His divine tasks, my service becomes imbued with a sense of exhilaration and fulfillment.

Calling protects your motives

Additionally, my telephone conversation serves to safeguard my intentions. At times, I find myself engaging in actions driven by impure motivations. While the enticement of financial gain may cross my mind, I am promptly reminded by a higher power that I have a divine calling. Although I may be inclined to appease others, I am constantly reminded by God that it is He who summoned me forth. Possessing a distinct sense of vocation serves as a safeguard to protect my heart against various erroneous motivations.

Undoubtedly, a strong sense of vocation is crucial for maintaining pure intentions. However, how does a leader discern and interpret the divine "calling" bestowed upon them by God? We regret to inform that this chapter does not allow for an exhaustive examination of the aforementioned issue, however, we deem it appropriate to offer a few observations. The majority of individuals will never encounter a profound and transformative epiphany akin to the apostle Paul's experience on the road to Damascus. However, certain Christian leaders do experience the divine "calling" of God through supernatural occurrences, which serve as a means of divine communication. For the majority, it is likely that Divine communication would manifest in less theatrical manners.

Certain individuals perceive the guidance of God in their existence as they cultivate their innate talents and remain steadfast in their devotion towards divine service within their respective circumstances. Gradually, they are being entrusted with increasingly significant responsibilities. On numerous occasions, the prospective leader fails to acknowledge their own capacity until external validation prompts them to contemplate assuming a leadership role. By engaging in prayer, contemplation, and seeking guidance from wise individuals, one can receive divine affirmation of their vocation.

Indeed, it is undeniably appropriate for fellow adherents to prompt an individual to contemplate the divine summons. Individuals are required to resolve the matter completely within themselves, independent of external viewpoints.

Numerous ecclesiastical authorities face an inherent inner conflict when it comes to discerning and reconciling with God's divine summons. They perceive a beckoning, yet it appears to be an immense undertaking or excessively expensive. They apprehend that it will result in their family enduring a life of destitution. When an individual is summoned by the divine to transition from the realm of familiarity to that of uncertainty, inevitable trepidation and inquiries shall arise. Decisions of this nature necessitate the contemplation of prayer, discerning guidance from individuals grounded in spiritual wisdom, and a deliberate investment of time. The duration dedicated to contemplation and discernment of God's calling is not futile. Divine intervention will cleanse your intentions and imbue you with unwavering determination, ensuring that you do not falter in the future. When one possesses the assurance that they are answering God's summons, they should embark upon the endeavor. Although the telephone conversation might have a high expense, it remains more economical compared to engaging in disobedient actions.

Similarly, it is imperative that leaders within the Christian community across various domains are unequivocally invited to assume their designated roles or vocations. Career decisions ought to be informed by a sense of divine guidance, rather than purely relying on the availability of opportunities or financial benefits.

Ultimately, it is imperative for all Christian leaders to confidently declare, "I am situated in my present leadership role as a result of God's divine purpose." Would you assert the same regarding your existing position of leadership?

The primary objective of the leader is to provide service.

According to Peter's perspective, our role can be described as "fulfilling the duties of supervisors." In contemporary language, we can interpret this as "exercising leadership through service." Although it may seem contradictory, this approach aligns with the principles of Christianity. Within society, as an individual ascends in their position of authority, an increasing number of individuals assume the responsibility of serving them. Contrarily, the situation is reversed in the Kingdom. Leaders are servants.

Jesus arrived in the role of a servant. He performed the act of cleansing and purifying the feet of His disciples, and now He urges us to assume a leadership role based on His exemplary conduct. "The primary purpose of the arrival of the son of man was not to obtain service, but rather to provide service and sacrifice his life as a means of redemption for numerous individuals" (Mark 10:45). This principle is relevant within the confines of one's household, as well as within the context of a church finance committee and in the corporate boardroom. As one ascends the hierarchy of leadership, their entitlements diminish while their obligations escalate. As you ascend to greater heights, the expectations placed upon you by others escalate. Your time transforms into their time; your resources morph into their resources.

Your life becomes transparent and easily accessible by others.

If you are not prepared to fulfill your duties in Christian leadership, kindly withdraw from your position. Examine your motives. Do you assume a leadership role with the intention of serving others, or with the intention of being served? Furthermore, it should be acknowledged that the author of this particular passage on leadership is none other than Peter, who, incidentally, engaged in a fervent debate about his own greatness during the last supper and hesitated to permit Jesus to cleanse his feet. The divine has the power to restore and metamorphose an individual.

Serving also implies the intention to provide, rather than receive. Peter warns against being overly covetous of wealth. The pursuit of material riches has derailed countless leaders within and beyond the confines of the church. Despite the absence of financial compensation accompanying your leadership role, you may still be inclined to serve due to the benefits it entails. You have the opportunity to acquire prestige, a distinguished position, an honorary designation, or public commendation. Experiencing power and authority can evoke a sense of gratification, leading many individuals to assume leadership positions.

Providing assistance necessitates an authentic display of affection. Love demonstrates concern for the well-being of others. Love exhibits a magnanimous spirit, desiring the success and advancement of others. To what extent do you possess affection and devotion for the individuals under your guidance?

All leaders are driven by the desire to either acquire or contribute. However, as per Peter's perspective, Christian leadership is distinguished by the act of giving rather than receiving. As a leader, it is incumbent upon me to allocate my time, financial resources, prayers, and affection in order to serve those who are under my care.

In order to bestow unto others, it is imperative that I acquire something in return. What is my source? God Himself. This represents a profound advantage of Christian leadership: the ability to transmit to others the blessings bestowed upon you by God. Leaders ought to approach the divine realm, seek guidance directly from the deity, and subsequently disseminate it among their subordinates. It is widely recognized that culinary delights are most savored within the confines of the kitchen, just as they emanate from the sound of the sizzling skillet, as opposed to when they are served subsequently. If I were a leader driven by the pursuit of serving and bestowing upon others, I would undoubtedly be granted this divine blessing by God. Do you consider your role as one of providing or receiving, serving or being served?

Establish a Strong Connection with the Workforce of the Millennial Generation

After implementing the revised work model, proceed to the subsequent stage of engaging with your Generation Y employees. This holds significant significance as the absence of interpersonal connectivity is the root cause of the disparities observed between different generations.

Establishing effective communication with your Generation Y workforce will facilitate mutual understanding and enhance engagement levels with your millennial employees. When employees develop a familiarity and rapport with one another, they gain insight into each other's needs and effectively adapt accordingly. This guarantees a continuous and upward trajectory of development and accomplishments within the organization.

In order to facilitate the continuous growth of your organization, it is imperative that you focus on enhancing your rapport with the Millennial workforce within your company.

Herein lies a collection of strategies and advice to assist you in attaining this objective.

Have Increased Face Time

An effective method to establish a stronger connection with your employees and gain deeper insights into their perspectives is to facilitate more opportunities for in-person interaction within the workplace. This necessitates regular meetings and engagement with them. Conducting regular meetings affords you the opportunity to provide them with frequent, direct interaction and ongoing feedback, thereby fostering increased engagement.

During your scheduled meetings, adapt a flexible and open-minded approach, engaging in polite and congenial interactions with your millennial subordinates. Millennials seek ongoing harmonious engagement with their superiors and are disinclined towards superiors who display obstinacy and rudeness, maintaining an air of unwavering omniscience. Demonstrate adaptability and establish meaningful connections with your millennial employees within a cordial environment. Should you choose to take action, it will prompt a reciprocation from them in the form of a heightened determination and intensified endeavors to make a favorable impression upon you.

Get Their Feedback

In addition to offering feedback to them, it is advisable to solicit feedback from the Millennials on your managerial endeavors and proficiency. Individuals belonging to the millennial generation derive satisfaction from both receiving and providing feedback. When offering feedback, your millennial employees will utilize it to enhance their performance. By requesting feedback from them regarding your demeanor, conduct, and leadership approach, you convey your desire to enhance your managerial abilities and foster a sense of ease within the organization. When convening a meeting with your millennial workforce, inquire about strategies for enhancing managerial skills, genuinely consider their suggestions, and actively incorporate them into practice.

Encourage employee involvement beyond the confines of the office

As stated by Alim Erginoglu of Towers Watson, an expert consultant in employee engagement, establishing a connection with employees necessitates actively involving them beyond the confines of the workplace. Effective employers establish strong connections and foster meaningful relationships with their millennial employees both within and beyond the confines of the workplace.

Assign your millennial employees with outdoor assignments and initiatives that necessitate them stepping away from the confines of the workplace, providing them with an opportunity to unwind and foster stronger connections. The workplace environment often becomes laden with significant levels of stress, impeding the ability for both you and your millennial workforce to establish meaningful rapport.

External commitments provide you and your millennial workforce with a chance to foster connections in an alternate setting. Additionally, it provides Millennials with an opportunity to engage in social interactions within novel settings, an experience that they greatly appreciate.

Gain Each Other's Trust

Establishing mutual trust and upholding it is an effective approach for fostering strong bonds with millennial employees. To establish trust, it is important to exhibit genuineness, transparency, and authenticity. Embrace authenticity when interacting with your Millennial employees, even if it means deviating from your desired demeanor.

As an illustration, supposing you possess a naturally amenable and relaxed demeanor in reality, but attempt to portray yourself as an exceptionally obstinate and indifferent superior who places little value on employees and insists on rigid compliance with rules, it is advisable to cease this artificial behavior and embrace your authentic self.

By exhibiting authenticity, you allow your millennial subordinates to gain insight into your genuine character and enhance their understanding of you. Furthermore, this aids in the cultivation of a connection founded on mutual trust and comprehension, allowing individuals to embrace their distinctive individuality.

Acknowledge their aptitude and intellectual capabilities.

In order to establish a strong connection with the Millennial cohort within your organization, aside from executing the aforementioned strategies, it is imperative to undertake an additional measure: acknowledge the inherent talent and intellect of millennials and effectively communicate your appreciation for their expertise, recognizing them as indispensable contributors.

When scheduling a meeting with your millennial employees, it is important to place emphasis on the competencies and abilities exhibited by this diligent generation, expressing gratitude for their contributions to the organization. If certain individuals from the Millennial generation encounter challenges in validating themselves, it is advisable to foster a culture of motivation by acknowledging their endeavors, imparting appreciation, and conveying unwavering support towards their journey of personal betterment.

As per the perspective of Nicole Cunningham, a senior manager at Knot Standard specializing in employee experiences, it can be observed that Millennials possess a strong inclination towards collaborative work within teams, while also exhibiting individual motivation. Employ a personalized approach to engage and inspire each of your Generation Y employees, thereby encouraging them to sustain their exemplary performance.

Coach your Millennials

An additional measure that must be taken to establish a connection with individuals belonging to the Millennial generation is the adoption of a leadership style that is centered around coaching. Individuals belonging to the millennial generation possess limited affinity towards autocratic regimes and the experience of being subjected to oppressive authority. If you persist in governing them with an authoritarian approach, the Millennials will ostracize you. Therefore, in order to cultivate a strong rapport with individuals belonging to the Millennial generation, assume the role of their mentor or guide.

Abandon your conventional approach to leadership and cease regarding yourself as their superior. Being a coach entails assuming the role of a mentor rather than an authoritarian figure, requiring one to display humility and gentleness.

Engage in the implementation of these strategies; by doing so, you and your millennial colleagues will cultivate a remarkable rapport, resulting in substantial advantages for your organization.

Equip Your Followers For Achieving Success

An unquestionably accurate statement would be: "Leadership fundamentally involves the cultivation and development of future exemplary leaders."

Build Self-Confidence in Others

A method to cultivate effective leaders is to foster their self-assurance. If you currently hold a leadership position, it is expected that you possess a certain level of self-assurance. If you found yourself thrust into this position without prior preparation and with a noticeable deficiency in confidence, it is imperative that you commence to cultivate this attribute within yourself. Assuming you possess an existing level of confidence and aim to enhance your leadership abilities, it would be advisable to focus on instilling confidence in others.

Strategies for instilling confidence in individuals as a means to foster leadership growth:
- Give more responsibility
- Express commendation for exceptional work performed
- Direct your attention to the positive attributes of every person
- Provide an opportunity for a team member to instruct someone else
- Foster positivity and impart knowledge to team members on transforming 'failures' into valuable opportunities for growth
- Offer guidance

Below are several methods to support team members in developing their confidence. The crucial aspect is to avoid putting your team in a position that guarantees failure. To achieve this, it is imperative to provide clear instructions regarding expectations and ensure that as their leader, you have fulfilled your responsibilities by effectively imparting the essential knowledge required for your team members to successfully tackle new tasks and overcome challenges.

Instruct individuals on cultivating qualities of collaboration and teamwork.

When occupying a position of leadership wherein the collaboration of one's team is imperative to attain shared organizational objectives, it is imperative to ensure that the team possesses the aptitude for collective effort. In the event that they do not possess such proficiency, it becomes incumbent upon you, as the leader, to impart upon them the ability to collaborate effectively.

Leadership Pointer #16: Strategies for imparting the importance of teamwork to others:

• Engage in open and transparent discussions with your team regarding the significance of collaboration. • Converse with your team honestly and openly about the relevance of working together. • Initiate sincere and straightforward conversations within your team, highlighting the value of collective effort. Perhaps it may come as a surprise to discover the considerable number of individuals who exhibit a reluctance to collaborate within a team setting and fail to perceive the inherent advantages.

- Reiterate the shared vision that guides the team's collaborative efforts
- Ensure that there are definite time limits for the tasks delegated to the team
- Ensure that each individual within the team has well-defined responsibilities.
- Approach individuals with respect for their unique attributes, recognizing the diverse personalities present within the team. Utilize this knowledge to meticulously assemble cohesive teams and assign roles strategically, aiming to maximize each individual's contributions within the team context.
- Conduct weekly follow-ups (or at a frequency that suits your preference) to address any concerns pertaining to the team's work progress.
- Commend employees for exemplary performance • Express appreciation for

successful completion of tasks
• Acknowledge and recognize achievements in the workplace
• Organize team bonding exercises; incorporating enjoyable activities both within and beyond the workplace can greatly contribute to fostering a more cohesive team.

One should refrain from attempting to compel individuals with inherently incompatible opinions and an inability to find common ground to collaborate. It is an inherent phenomenon: interpersonal compatibility cannot be universally attained.

When assembling your teams, it is advisable to group individuals who foster a conducive environment that nurtures one another's growth and brings forth their utmost potential as cohesive team members. In this manner, they will consistently be motivated to substantiate their assertions to the opposing teams. By implementing this approach, you can foster a culture of constructive competition in the workplace, particularly when overseeing a business enterprise that is sensitive to turnover and performance outcomes.

Allow teams to select their own leaders: While there may not be any inherent issues with designating team leaders for each created team, to strengthen team cohesion and enhance overall effectiveness, it is beneficial to grant the autonomy for individual teams to choose their own leaders.

Members of the team likely possess a deeper understanding of each other's competencies and limitations, thereby enabling them to make well-informed decisions regarding the most adept and capable individual to assume a leadership role.

Establish recurring objectives: Teams should consistently commit to targets: something to strive for. Hence, establish immediate objectives for every team. In this manner, your followers will cultivate assurance as they achieve each significant progress.

Objectives have a tendency to inspire individuals to showcase their utmost capabilities, particularly when team members are aware of their collective responsibility in contributing towards the achievement of the set target.

Provide Encouragement: Offering incentives serves as an additional source of drive for the teams. Objectives and milestones gain an enhanced level of appeal in the presence of rewards for each accomplished endeavor.

Observe your team members diligently working extra hours with enthusiasm to accomplish a goal, motivated by a compelling incentive.

One could pursue a more advanced approach by implementing a system of incentives for the winning team and rewarding the most outstanding team member with a prize.

Adhering to these procedures will guarantee that every individual under your guidance acquires the necessary skills to make substantial contributions within a team context and progress towards the attainment of shared objectives.

Treat Everyone With Respect

Indeed, we previously discussed the notion of demonstrating respect; however, its significance is heightened within the framework of fostering confidence and teamwork among your team, which compelled me to reiterate its importance.

Unless you come to a juncture where you acknowledge the inherent worth of every member within your team, and demonstrate respect, courtesy, kindness, and understanding towards them, your ability to exhibit influential leadership will remain unattainable.

Leadership Recommendation #17: Effectively Demonstrating Respect to Your Team Members

• Extend an opportunity for dialogue: Afford your team members the chance to express their perspectives, demonstrating that you place high regard on their thoughts and opinions. Show equal understanding and empathy when a team member approaches you with a personal matter as you would in the case of a professional issue.

- Retain the names and particulars of your subordinates: Demonstrating a genuine interest in their individuality signifies your appreciation for them - though this may prove challenging given the magnitude of your team, make an utmost effort at all times.
- Do not embody the type of leader who assumes a god-like status: It is important to humbly acknowledge all individuals within your organization whom you encounter, regardless of their position. Always greet them cordially, offer a genuine smile, and engage in pleasant interactions.
- Demonstrate genuine concern for their well-being: By taking the initiative to inquire about their welfare, you convey the message that you genuinely care about your team members, leading to an increased level of respect towards you.
- Express appreciation and accolades for the hard work and accomplishments of your team members: Positive reinforcement is highly effective in motivating and inspiring individuals.

Empower Your Followers

An additional method to exert a lasting impact on the lives of the individuals under your leadership is by bestowing them with the ability to influence and assisting them in developing their own influential capabilities. Certain individuals may employ various self-empowerment methods, yet certain adherents may require individualized assistance and guidance in order to optimize their capabilities.

As a proficient leader, it is imperative that you foster the growth of others by aiding them in unleashing their latent abilities and untapped potential.

Leadership Principle #18: Foster the empowerment of individuals in your vicinity:

- Assign critical responsibilities to team members: Demonstrate your confidence in their capabilities to effectively undertake these tasks; one can never truly ascertain someone's potential until they are granted an opportunity

- Ensure the consultation of your team and actively engage them in the decision-making process to the greatest extent possible: It is important to recognize that certain team members may have more experience within the company than you do. Do not hesitate to solicit their input; doing so will not diminish your effectiveness as a leader. Indeed, it enhances and cultivates the confidence of your followers in addition to fostering your own capacity for leadership.
- Implement the advice provided: The primary purpose of seeking guidance is to acquire insights or discover improved methods for addressing encountered difficulties. Therefore, once you receive a valuable suggestion, it would be beneficial to put it into action. By doing so, you will empower the team member to generate further beneficial ideas.
- Acknowledge the contributions of others: When you adopt a suggestion from a subordinate, ensure proper recognition is given; this cultivates trust

within your team and reflects your leadership capacity to not only adopt valuable ideas from others but also acknowledge and reward them accordingly.

Develop Your Followers

The simultaneous cultivation and empowerment of your subordinates are inherently interrelated. In aspiring to become a transformative leader, it is imperative to actively seek avenues for nurturing the growth and harnessing the full potential of the individuals under your guidance.

Leadership Strategy #19: Strategies for Cultivating the Growth and Development of Your Subordinates

• Facilitate the organization of seminars and webinars: It is important not to underestimate the value of continuous learning for your team, even if they have been in their current roles for an extended period. By providing them with opportunities to acquire new knowledge and skills, not only will they be able to enhance their performance in their current roles, but they will also be better equipped to progress in their careers. Ongoing education can also sustain enthusiasm and dedication for one's profession.

• Connect with individuals who have specialized in specific fields and extend an invitation for them to share their expertise and insights with your team. For example, consider engaging a renowned software expert to deliver a presentation to your IT team regarding the most recent technological application in the industry. Furthermore, you have the option of engaging a business coach who can impart contemporary principles of business ethics to your team, as an illustration.

• Elaborate on this idea and consider including individuals to engage in discussions about topics that might not immediately appear directly related to work. For instance, a proficient fitness or nutritionist specialist, or an astute investor, who can provide insights into the fundamental principles of money investment. It is imperative to bear in mind that employees who are content and in good health tend to exhibit greater levels of productivity.

Instructing Others in the Pursuit of Excellence

In your role as a proficient leader, it is incumbent upon you to motivate your subordinates to pursue excellence in all facets of their existence. Assist your followers in comprehending the long-term benefits of striving for excellence.

Your subordinates may find it convenient to take shortcuts while striving to meet deadlines, which often leads to subpar outcomes. Impart this important message to your followers: Success is never attained through mediocrity. Imbue the essence of exceptionalism by embodying excellence in all of your endeavors.

"Leadership Advice #20 Promote the cultivation of excellence through consistent embodiment:

- Develop a clear vision and establish goals

- Acquire additional competencies
- Enhance one's skill set
- Foster skill development
- Offer selflessly
- Provide without anticipating reciprocation
- Extend generosity without any ulterior motives
- Offer assistance unconditionally
- Teach others
- Engage in introspection to identify your own restricting beliefs
- Volunteer
- Exercise daily
- Enhance your existing strengths
- Encourage others
- Show empathy towards others
- Strive to maintain justice and fairness in all your transactions
- Uphold the principles of equity and fairness in every business endeavor
- Ensure that all your interactions are characterized by impartiality and fairness
- Conduct yourself with integrity and fairness in all your professional interactions
- Seek to establish a reputation for equity and fairness in every aspect of your dealings
- Pay heed to the perspectives of others

- Complete a task without expressing dissatisfaction.
- Embrace a fervent approach when engaging in all endeavors
- Identify the positive attributes in others
- Engage in the perusal of significant literary materials
- Seek counsel • Request guidance • Solicit recommendations
- Find a mentor

The aforementioned list is not exhaustive. There exist numerous avenues through which one can strive for greatness, enhancing one's own capabilities while simultaneously serving as a source of inspiration and a role model for others. I strongly urge you to explore and embrace all such opportunities. However, if you are engaging in even a handful of the activities outlined above, it is evident that you are making significant progress.

Instructing individuals under your guidance on the path to achieving excellence necessitates upholding an unwavering personal benchmark in all of your endeavors; effectively communicating and demonstrating these standards holds utmost importance.

Increase Influence

It is imperative for a leader to possess the ability to exert influence upon their followers, and potentially, individuals beyond their immediate sphere of influence. Conveying ideas and delivering speeches might come effortlessly to some; however, retaining a lasting influence on individuals and preventing them from readily dismissing your words can prove to be a more challenging endeavor.

In the capacity of a leader, it is crucial to acknowledge that your words possess the potential to profoundly influence individuals' lives, serving as a driving force for transformation. But may I inquire how you can ascertain that you are manifesting as an affirmative catalyst and that your impact shall endure? Peruse these guidelines and ascertain.

Initially, acquaint yourself with your own identity. As previously stated, it is paramount to possess self-awareness in order to excel as a leader and wield influence effectively. If one is uncertain about their own identity and aspirations, commanding the attention and respect of others becomes an improbable feat. Acquaint yourself with your strengths, while simultaneously familiarizing yourself with your weaknesses, thereby preventing others from exploiting or subjecting you to ridicule based on them. Do you find it effortless to win over individuals through the use of your smile and conversational skills? Make use of it. Do you possess the inclination to captivate individuals through a refined appearance and articulate communication that reflects a professional demeanor? Good for you.

Having an understanding of the ways in which you can exert influence over others will facilitate your ability to effectively communicate your ideas and have them attentively listened to.

Be assertive. It is not considered inappropriate to exhibit assertiveness and employ persuasive techniques to captivate individuals, compelling them to give due consideration to your perspectives. Why? On occasion, it becomes imperative to engage with individuals directly in order to capture their attention instead of relying on their willingness to attentively listen to you. You will refrain from boasting about your knowledge or attempting to impose your desired understanding on others. Instead, you will captivate their attention through assertiveness, creating an impression that your words carry significance and should be heard. It is equally acceptable for you to question the perspectives of others as it fosters a constructive dialogue on the necessary course of action. Do not hesitate to voice your thoughts/opinions.

Be logical. To gain credibility in one's ideas, it is imperative to demonstrate both rationality and logical thinking, along with the vindication of presenting these ideas with sound reasoning. It is imperative to strategize and articulate your thoughts with appropriate finesse. Instead of merely engaging in conversation, consider producing a Powerpoint Presentation or even crafting a video to effectively articulate your thoughts and ideas. If you desire individuals to lend their ears to your voice, ensure that your intentions are lucid and exempt from any signs of amateurishness.

Learn how to negotiate. Naturally, it is to be anticipated that not everyone will instantaneously embrace your ideas, and acquiring favorable outcomes will require more than a mere flick of the wrist. The critical factor for achieving success in this context lies in acquiring the skills of effective communication, negotiation, and, when appropriate, the ability to reach compromises. In this manner, you can also lend an ear to the viewpoints of others instead of exclusively advocating for your own ideas. Furthermore, acquiring skills in negotiation would undoubtedly empower you to secure exceptional bargains.

Bridge the gap. Comprehend individuals' requisites and absences thereof. Acquire an understanding of the reasons behind their inclination to favor a specific product and the rationale behind their probable disregard for others, and proceed to address those factors. Understanding oneself and comprehending the individuals in one's surroundings, as well as their cultural background, is essential. By doing so, it becomes effortless to align one's actions with people's desires and effectively cater to their needs. Determine your areas of proficiency and identify the areas where improvement is needed. Do not attempt to amend something that is not flawed; instead, focus your efforts on rectifying any existing issues, paving the path towards achieving success. Formulate effective strategies and arrange team-based initiatives or workshops to ensure a collective understanding and involvement in order to execute tasks proficiently, not solely reliant on your knowledge.

Comprehension is facilitated when individuals are able to relate concepts to practical situations in the real world. This is because they possess a comprehensive understanding of the significance of this product or service. In this manner, there is potential for an expansion of your influence as individuals engage in discussions regarding your accomplishments and come to recognize the profound impact it has on their lives.

Exhibit the qualities that would inspire others to willingly become your followers. How? Exert relentless effort and demonstrate that your position as a leader does not entail idleness, rather it signifies a commitment to actively engage in laborious tasks alongside your subordinates. Exemplify diligent efforts in order to empower and motivate others to exert diligent efforts as well. Undoubtedly, implementing this approach would greatly enhance the working environment.

It is important to bear in mind that practice is crucial for achieving perfection. It is a commonly used phrase, yet it holds truth. As previously mentioned, conducting market tests will enable you to determine the viability of producing specific products or services, as well as gauge consumer preferences towards them. Establish a clear determination of your intended target demographic and direct your focus exclusively towards that grouping—at least for the time being. It is more efficient to conduct market tests with a small group of individuals rather than attempting to reach a broad audience and obtaining inconclusive outcomes. Commence with modest beginnings as, in due time, the returns shall witness considerable expansion.

It is imperative to establish well-defined objectives and a clear vision for the future. Is it not true that individuals are typically inquired about their future objectives when they submit a job application? Certainly, your audience would undoubtedly be interested in being informed about the objectives you have set for the forthcoming time as well. By adopting this approach, it would communicate your confidence in your decision-making ability and affirm that they are indeed affiliated with a reputable and secure organization. By adopting this approach, you will witness a significant expansion of your impact while alleviating any concerns about the future they may have.

Transforming Pessimistic Thoughts Into Optimistic Perspectives

Human cognition can be categorized into two fundamental perspectives, namely perceiving the glass as half full or perceiving the glass as half empty. This fundamentally indicates that you perceive life through either an optimistic or pessimistic lens. Individuals who hold the belief that the glass is half full generally possess an optimistic outlook on life. Individuals who perceive the glass to be half empty typically display a pessimistic outlook. While anger is a universal emotion that people encounter in their lives, individuals with a propensity to perceive the negative aspects of situations may undergo heightened levels of anger. However, it should be noted that this is not an absolute or inflexible principle. Positive-minded individuals may also experience difficulty in managing intense aggression.

In the presence of persistent negative thoughts in one's mind, it becomes challenging to discern the positive aspects in any given situation. It is possible that you have consistently encountered disenchantment on multiple occasions. Alternatively, you may perceive that you have been subjected to unfortunate circumstances in your journey through life. It is challenging to rid oneself of such thoughts. They brood within the psyche and manifest in nearly every circumstance one confronts. Unfortunately, negativity breeds negativity. Once you cultivate an awareness and comprehension of your negative thoughts, you can commence transforming these detrimental thoughts into ones of a more positive nature.

There are numerous factors that might compel you to contemplate adopting a new perspective. To begin with, residing in a state of negativity can lead to significant physical and mental fatigue. The act of being pessimistic requires significantly more emotional and mental energy compared to maintaining a positive outlook. Furthermore, it can potentially give rise to considerable health complications. Adverse mental patterns can also contribute to challenges in fostering healthy interpersonal connections. Moreover, they have the potential to generate discord among your colleagues. Interacting with an individual who consistently perceives the negative aspects can be exceptionally tiresome. You may observe individuals exhibiting a tendency to create distance from your person. If any or a selection of these circumstances resonate with your current situation, making the effort to alter your mindset could prove beneficial for your well-being.

Ten Strategies for Achieving a Positive Mindset Transformation

There exist various approaches that one can employ to facilitate the conversion of negative thought patterns into positive ones. Each individual possesses unique characteristics, thus strategies or methods that prove effective for certain individuals may not yield similar results for others. You might discover that a particular approach proves especially beneficial, or alternatively, you might realize the necessity of utilizing multiple methods. Irrespective of one's personal circumstances, it is imperative to bear in mind that this endeavor will require considerable effort. This endeavor will require a substantial investment of both time and effort. There may arise occasions where you achieve significant success, coupled with occasional instances of failure. All of that is acceptable, all of that is within the realm of the customary. In instances of committing errors, refrain from relinquishing your pursuit. Rather, allow yourself to experience the sentiment of disappointment, gather your composure, and make another attempt. Presented below are ten strategies that can be employed to transform negative thoughts into more positive perspectives.

Exercise

Engaging in physical activity is an excellent method for relieving stress. One can release any accumulated energy by engaging in activities such as visiting the gym, jogging around the neighborhood, or participating in a basketball session. Even if you are in the contrary situation and consistently experience fatigue, physical activity remains beneficial. Contrary to initial intuition, engaging in physical activity serves to amplify energy levels rather than deplete them. Exercise also releases endorphins. Endorphins are among the euphoria-inducing hormones that are naturally synthesized within the human body. When engaging in physical activity, it is possible to experience an immediate improvement in one's emotional state regarding a specific circumstance.

While physical activity is commonly associated with attending fitness facilities, numerous alternatives exist to engage in a comprehensive workout. Please select something that provides you with a sense of comfort. If you prefer an individual setting, consider engaging in exercise within the confines of your residence or secluded outdoor area. There is a plethora of instructional workout videos available for use in the comfort of your own home. If you possess a penchant for sociability, consider enrolling in a regular league catered to your preferred sport. Select the activity or activities that most appropriately align with your preferences. Engaging in activities that bring you enjoyment is the most effective approach to achieving desired outcomes.

Meditation or Yoga

Practices such as meditation or yoga primarily involve the directed concentration of one's mind. Both of these techniques promote the cultivation of attentiveness towards one's physical sensations and respiratory patterns. This serves as a distraction from any challenges that may be present in your life. It is beneficial to provide respite for your mind through maintaining mindfulness. Your concerns, anxieties, and frustrations are alleviated, if only temporarily. Upon the conclusion of a session, you might be pleasantly astonished by the profound tranquility you experience.

There exist numerous methods through which one can actively participate in the practices of meditation or yoga. You have the option to enroll in a class at a nearby studio or fitness center. Numerous major urban centers provide complimentary yoga sessions in the park if you seek a more economical option. Conduct some preliminary investigation and ascertain the available options within your locality. If you have a preference for individual practice, you could consider exploring yoga videos or utilizing yoga applications. In this manner, you can partake in a guided yoga session within the confines of your personal residence. In addition, one can avail oneself of mobile applications and instructional videos specifically designed for the purpose of practicing meditation. Do not hesitate to test out multiple options until you discover one that suits your needs.

Steer clear of individuals with a negative disposition and seek out those with a positive mindset.

Pessimism has the tendency to fuel further pessimism. On subsequent occasions when you find yourself in the company of your friends or colleagues, diligently observe and listen to the content of their conversations. Ascertain whether their tone and subjects of discourse predominantly exhibit pessimistic or optimistic perspectives. If the sentiments expressed are unfavorable, we ask that you kindly excuse yourself from the discussion. Associating oneself with individuals who exhibit a pessimistic outlook will solely serve to intensify one's own negative disposition.

Make a concerted effort to associate yourself with individuals who possess a more optimistic disposition. Initially, this may appear overwhelming. At times, individuals may find themselves irked by individuals who consistently display an unwavering positive demeanor. Upon acquainting yourself with them for a period, you might discover the permeating influence of their attitude.

Make Yourself Smile

Although this suggestion may appear peculiar, it is indeed effective. Exerting oneself to maintain a smile is akin to intentionally cultivating a state of happiness. Please proceed to the restroom and avail yourself of the opportunity to view your reflection in the mirror. Adorn yourself with your most radiant smile and witness the beauty it bestows upon you. Individuals appear most appealing when they exhibit a cheerful countenance. It exudes an aura of warmth, friendliness, and approachability. All of these characteristics are deemed desirable.

Upon the acquisition of self-assurance in your smile, proceed to showcase it in public. In your future interactions, endeavor to greet others cordially by extending a warm salutation accompanied by a pleasant facial expression. Throughout the course of the dialogue, it is advised to maintain a pleasant and courteous facial expression when discussing matters of positive nature. Smiling, perhaps, represents a conditioned reaction to various situations in your case. It may also require some diligent effort. After acquiring proficiency, one may be astonished by the efficacy of wearing a smile, as it can effectively diminish the adverse thoughts plaguing one's mind.

Offer Your Time and Expertise as a Volunteer

Assisting others is a well-established method to transform pessimistic thoughts into optimistic ones. In addition to diverting your attention from personal challenges, engaging in this activity fosters a heightened awareness of others' potentially more arduous circumstances. It can evoke a sense of gratitude for one's blessings. Moreover, bringing a smile to someone's face or alleviating their stress will imbue you with a profound sense of joy.

Seize Command over Your Existence

Your pessimism may arise from a perception that unfortunate events consistently befall you. In the event that this is indeed true, desist from assuming a role of victimhood. Acquire the ability to assume command of your life and effectively manage the circumstances you come across. Do not allow yourself to be taken advantage of. Initially, advocating for oneself might pose a challenge, but with progressive experience, it will become increasingly effortless. Summon the bravery to prioritize your own needs and observe how your negative thoughts metamorphose into positive ones.

Engage in Truthfulness and Transparency with Individuals whom You Hold in High Esteem.
Incorporating the perspectives and considerations of others into your thought process can assist in ensuring that you remain aligned with the correct course. Inform them that you are implementing measures to address and alleviate your anger, as well as minimize any negative emotions. This will prove to be highly advantageous in situations that give rise to triggering events. Your trusted companions will exhibit greater levels of tolerance towards you and can assist you in handling instances of emotional distress. Additionally, they have the ability to identify instances where you may unknowingly convey negativity.

Alter the Attitude of Your Mindset

Pervasive negativity resides within the depths of your mind. Develop a mindset that reframes unfavorable circumstances in a more constructive manner. As an illustration, should you be assigned a task at your workplace that is not particularly appealing to you, it may be inherent in your disposition to seek solace in sharing your grievances with colleagues. Alternatively, reframe your perspective to acknowledge that your boss assigned you this task to facilitate the development of your proficiency. Accomplishing the task proficiently can facilitate your progression in your professional trajectory. Reiterate to yourself the importance of maintaining a positive mindset with regularity. It will require effort, but over time, your thoughts will naturally transition to a more positive mindset.

Read Inspirational Quotes

Conduct thorough research and compile a collection of quotations that resonate with your personal values and beliefs. They may consist of quotations from your preferred motion picture, authored by a renowned writer, or even derived from an internet meme. The only thing of significance is that the words resonate with you. Following that, proceed to display the quote in a location that you frequently observe on a daily basis. Placing the quotes on your mirror, computer screen, or wallet would be an excellent choice. Consult the quotation for a source of invigorating positivity as required. It is possible that you will experience a sense of improvement simply by engaging in the act of reading those words.

Seek Professional Help

If you determine that none of these strategies prove effective in altering your mindset, it may be advisable to seek guidance from a qualified professional. There is no humiliation in collaborating with a certified professional in the field of mental health. If you harbor reservations about engaging in face-to-face interactions, there exists a multitude of online counselors accessible and accessible for your benefit. The social stigma associated with engaging in psychotherapy is gradually receding, thus there should be no impediment to seeking professional assistance whenever required.

www.ingramcontent.com/pod-product-compliance
Lightning Source LLC
Chambersburg PA
CBHW050026130526
44590CB00042B/1969